Introduction

THE LOST ART OF FA

> These commandments that I give you today are to be on
> your hearts. Impress them on your children. Talk about
> them when you sit at home and when you walk along
> the road, when you lie down and when you get up.
> Deuteronomy 6:6-7

We live in an age where more and more of our children are drifting away from the Christian faith. A recent study has shown that the majority of young people in Britain today identify as 'non religious', while a significant percentage of those brought up in Christian homes reject Christianity as they reach adulthood.[1] It is true that 'God has no grandchildren,' but something is wrong if the majority of those who grow up in the church end up leaving it.

While there is a variety of ways the church might respond to the loss of its youth, one of the key means is through the *recovery of family worship*. Worshipping together as a family, after all, is what God calls us to do. And it's something that Christian families have done together throughout history.

And yet the practice of family worship has become a lost art for many within the church. What was once common within Christian families is now rare, and family worship is seldom addressed by church leaders.[2] Recent research in the Church of England shows that many Christian parents do not see passing on their faith as a priority,[3] and even evangelical Christians struggle to keep this central.[4]

In the light of this loss, the aim of *Together with God* is to inspire and encourage Christian parents to begin or continue family worship within their homes. Rather than giving a precise guide or description of what families should do in worshipping together, *Together with God* offers a basic introduction to family worship – what it is and why it's important – alongside 15 stories of families from a variety of backgrounds worshipping God together at home.

We've had the privilege of collecting these stories from interviews with families from across the United Kingdom. While each family is different, they all share a commitment to helping their children learn to love and to trust God. Each family shared their joys as well as their struggles, while also offering tips for those wishing to start family worship.

Our hope is that you will find in these stories ideas for developing a way of worshipping together that suits your family – whatever its shape and size. It may be that you're happily married with one child, or a single parent raising three, or a Christian married to a non-Christian spouse.[5] Although the challenges will be different in each case, you'll find ideas here that you can adapt for your own context. The final chapter will offer advice for getting started, as well as pointing you to further resources to help you lead family worship.

WHAT IS FAMILY WORSHIP?

Christians – including Christian families – are called to worship God in the *whole* of life (Rom 12:1-2). All of life is to be lived following Jesus as Lord, and so worship should permeate all that we do and say. 'Family worship', however, can also be used to describe those intentional times when families gather together to encounter God. And families do so in a huge variety of ways.

Some families use arts and crafts, while others focus on engaging discussions; some follow a clear and systematic format, while others are far more fluid in their approach; some sing and others spend time in silence. Families are different, and different families need to find a way of worshipping God that suits them.

Despite this variety, there are two key elements of family worship that should always be there; *listening* to God and *talking* to God.

Listening to God takes place when we read the Bible and listen to its teachings. The Bible is the 'Word of God,' the 'living and breathing' Word that can really change us (2 Tim 3:16; Heb 4:12). It's the place where we encounter God. Even though the Spirit might prompt and speak to us in other ways, it's primarily through the Bible that God engages us.[6]

Talking to God involves prayer. Prayer includes thanksgiving, intercession, confession, and even 'lament' (telling God why things are so hard and difficult). Prayer is important because it connects us to God. And teaching children to pray – just as Jesus taught his disciples to pray (Luke 11:1-13) – is one of the best lessons we can give them.

Family worship isn't a new idea. It's an ancient idea found in the Bible and practised throughout church history – and understanding where it comes from can also help us recover it for today.

FAMILY WORSHIP IN THE BIBLE

In the Bible, families have a crucial role in helping children grow in faith, with parents given the responsibility of bringing up their children to love and serve God.[7] Family worship is one of the key ways in which this can take place.

One of the clearest passages on this theme is found in Deuteronomy 6;

Hear, O Israel: The LORD our God, the LORD is one. Love the LORD your God with all your heart and with all your soul and with all your strength. These commandments that I give you today are to be on your hearts. Impress them on your children. Talk about them when you sit at home and when you walk along the road, when you lie down and when you get up. Tie them as symbols on your hands and bind them on your foreheads. Write them on the door frames of your houses and on your gates. Deuteronomy 6:4-9

The people of God are called to *immerse* themselves and their families in the law and instructions of God.[8] The words of God should shape every area of life, whether at home or on the road, in work or at play. Parents are encouraged to help children understand that all of life comes under God's guidance.

Reflecting a similar theme in the New Testament, Paul gives the following instruction;

Fathers, do not exasperate your children; instead, bring them up in the training and instruction of the Lord.
Ephesians 6:4

Paul focuses on the responsibility of the father, but it is one which mums as well as dads need to take seriously. To train and instruct children 'in the Lord' means that we help our children learn what it means to follow and love Jesus, to serve Jesus as Lord of all their life.[9]

While Deuteronomy 6 and Ephesians 6 suggest that family worship is concerned with *instruction* in the faith, the Bible always connects knowing the truths of the faith with the *worship and obedience of God*. In Psalm 78, the people of God are encouraged to tell the next generation about God's works so that those who hear might, 'put their trust in God and... keep his commands' (v. 7). If our knowledge of God does not lead to obedience, it is dead and even dangerous (James 2:19). The knowledge our children gain of God should flow into worship and a transformed life.

While we want to stress the importance of family worship in every Christian home, the Bible also shows that this sits alongside the church as the wider 'family of faith.'[10] All who follow Jesus are brothers and sisters to one another (Jam 2:14-17), following the same Lord and worshipping the same Father (Eph 4:4-6; 1 John 3:1-3). Christian families gather together with their church and in that gathering also encounter God. Family worship should be seen as a *complement* of church worship rather than its *replacement*.

Family worship can be difficult in homes where one spouse is not a Christian. Paul, however, encourages such parents that they too can influence their children as well as their spouse (1 Cor 7:14-16).[11] Mums and dads can pray for God's work within their home, reflecting God's love in their relationship to their husband or wife as well as with their kids.

We believe in family worship, then, because the Bible emphasises it. Parents are called to help their children learn what it means to live for God. While this includes a focus on teaching children about who God is and what He has done, its purpose is that the next generation will come to worship and love God with all their hearts and souls, minds and strength (Mark 12:28-34).

FAMILY WORSHIP IN HISTORY

In the history of the church, family worship has also allowed Christians at different times and places to keep their faith and pass it to their children. In fact, the call to nurture faith within families runs like a golden thread throughout the history of the church.[12]

In the early Church, writers such as Polycarp and Clement encouraged parents to take responsibility for their children's spiritual welfare.[13] John Chrysostom even wrote a whole treatise on the topic, encouraging Christian parents to see themselves as artists whose call is to fashion 'wondrous statues for God.'[14]

After a period of decline in the medieval era, family worship became a key emphasis again during the Reformation.[15] In the 16th century, Martin Luther wrote a short catechism – a series of questions and answers about the Christian faith – for parents to use with their children.[16] Calvin similarly encouraged parents to take a key role in teaching the faith at home, and the stress on educating children – in the home as well as in wider society – became characteristic within Protestant churches.

Family worship was also emphasised by the Puritans of the 17th century. As well as seeing the home as central for Christian formation, the Puritans preached regularly on the importance of family prayer and Bible reading.[17]

While the 18th and 19th century saw a decline in family worship – due in part to dads working increasingly away from the home – figures such as John Wesley and George Whitefield encouraged its revival. In the 19th century, J. C. Ryle, the Bishop of Liverpool, similarly called parents to raise children 'in the instruction of the Lord', and his sermon on *The Duties of Parents* continues to be influential today.[18]

While the 20th and 21st centuries have seen a decline in family worship among Christians, there are many working to retrieve and encourage the practice. A range of resources are available for parents wishing to begin praying and reading Scripture with their kids.[19] Hearing and sharing stories of what works well in different families is also a key way to help parents find ways of worship that fit their own context.

FAMILY WORSHIP TODAY

The following 15 chapters illustrate the range of ways in which families worship together. While the Bible and prayer remain central for each of the families featured, there is a great deal of variety in what they do. The families featured also come from a wide range of backgrounds – culturally and geographically – and worship at a range of different churches.

Each chapter offers a description of how the family worships together, and – where relevant – lists the resources that they have found helpful.[20] Each family also shares some of the benefits and challenges they have faced, as well offering advice for those thinking of starting family worship.

Family worship isn't always easy, but our conviction – and the conviction shared by the families within these pages – is that God works through families worshipping together, helping the next generation discover the love and the grace of Jesus.

The concluding chapter will offer some practical guidelines for starting or continuing family worship in your home. We'll also give a list of resources to help in family worship and seek to answer common questions parents raise. We'll end with a brief reflection on the *joy* of family worship.

THE STORIES

A culture of worship

'We want our boys to understand that if we don't understand the Bible, we don't understand God.'

Tuan Jin (TJ) and Narisa, and their sons Daniel and Gideon (aged 11 & 9), are a Southeast Asian family living in North London. They arrived separately in the UK as students in 1996, and met and married here. Originally from Buddhist and atheist families, they came to faith in their teenage and student years. They both work full time and now attend an Anglican church.

How do we worship together?

The family worships together in the evening in an informal and unstructured way. They read a chapter of the Bible together, with TJ and Narisa pointing out significant points and asking their sons questions about the passage.

The family started reading through the Bible at Genesis and is now up to Nehemiah.

> 'We don't want to skip bits that might be hard to understand, or topics that might be embarrassing; we want our boys to hear things from us first rather than others.'

TJ leaves for work early and works a long day, so the family worships together when he gets home.

> 'TJ wants to be involved and so it has to happen in the evening when he's around or during the weekends.'

After the discussion, TJ prays, followed by the boys, who pray a 'thank you' prayer and a 'request' prayer. Prayer and praise happen more spontaneously as well; Narisa will pray with the boys in the car to and from school, and often the boys will join in worship songs when TJ is practising the guitar for Sunday worship at church.

What's been challenging?

- Time.
'With both of us working and with after school activities for the boys, if we didn't make this a habit it simply would not work.'

- A lack of apparent progress.

'Sometimes it seems as if nothing is sinking in, but we pray it is an investment for the future.'

- Unanswered prayer.

'Sometimes God answers our prayers wondrously, but at other times we wait for a long time and need to explain to our boys that our ways are not God's ways.'

What's worked well?

- Laying a foundation.

'Daniel is now reading the Bible for himself and as he encounters different views and explores the world, we pray that these family worship times have equipped him for that.'

- A mark of distinction.

'It's helped us develop a family culture that is Christian, so it isn't a shock to them when they see we are different from the surrounding culture.'

- Learning from our children.

'The benefit of a free flowing unstructured devotional time is that our boys come up with things that we had not even thought of, which means we are as blessed by this as they are.'

Advice for getting started

- Start with yourself.

'To help your family understand God and love him, you need to do it yourself. They will pick up on hypocrisy, so spend time one to one with God each day yourself.'

- Easy things first.

'If your children are young then start by praying short prayers as you go along and sing along to worship songs. Then when you read the Bible together, maybe start with the easier stories and a good storybook Bible.'

- Pray.

'Don't do this in your own strength; whether you're struggling or not, ask God for his help.'

- Ask for help.

'When having a baby you often receive support from others, so why not do something similar with our spiritual lives?'

A pattern of prayer

'I feel that praying together regularly has fostered a closer bond between us; praying together establishes closeness between people.'

Catherine lives in Manchester with her two daughters, Carmen (aged 12) and Rosalia (aged 9). They are part of an Anglican church on the West side of Manchester.

How do we worship together?

Catherine and her girls have read a variety of Bibles and prayed together over the years. In the last few years they have developed a particular pattern of praying together each evening before bed.

'We don't do it every single evening but it is part of our routine; it's a pattern that we're used to.'

In the past they have found making up sung prayers a fun and engaging way to pray; one person would make up a tune and a short prayer and the other two would copy it. As the girls have got older, they have settled into the pattern of 'teaspoon' prayers.

'Teaspoon prayers follow a simple formula of TSP – Thank you, Sorry, Please. We sit together, usually in bed, and take turns to pray, using the teaspoon format. Sometimes we each thank God for one thing, then keep on going round till we've thanked God for all the things we want to that day; after that we move on to saying sorry for things that have made God sad; finally asking him for things, saying please, keeping going round and round until we've finished.'

They often use the please part to ask God to help grow the fruits of the Spirit in them so that they can improve on the things for which they've just said sorry.

'We still sometimes sing the Fruits of the Spirit song.'

What's been challenging?

- Things changing as the girls get older.

'As the girls get older they've not been so keen on some of the things we did when they were younger. We don't do the singing prayers anymore and sometimes one of them might want to pray in her head and not out loud.'

- Life situations.

'I was seriously ill last year and it has been physically exhausting to go back to work. Being on my own with the girls also adds to me being physically and emotionally tired. This can make carrying on with these things hard, but then again it makes it all the more important.'

What's worked well?

- The routine of the pattern.

'Having a regular time and place and format means it is easy for us to do each evening before bed. That has certainly made it easier to persevere over the longer term.'

- The flexibility of TSP prayers.

'With the TSP approach you can be as long and detailed or as short as you want. Sometimes we're done in a minute or two, but sometimes it goes on for much longer.'

- It helps reflection and discussion.

'In our times together we reflect on our day, but it also opens up opportunities to talk about all sorts of issues, some of which are quite grown up, like how we should pray for and then act towards those who have far less materially than us.'

- It helps me as the adult.

'This isn't just about the benefit to the children – I benefit too. It makes me reflect on my day spiritually and articulate my thanks and praise to God, as well as confessing my sin to him.'

Advice for getting started

- Keep it simple and flexible.

'The simple yet flexible pattern makes it easy for you and your children to engage and persevere.'

- Be realistic.

'Don't beat yourself up if you don't manage to do it every day.'

- Don't push it with your children.

'It's good to do all you can to encourage your children and make it accessible and engaging, but at the end of the day if they don't want to do it then pushing them will be counter-productive.'

Being in Christ, together

'I don't want them to get to a point where they're unable to speak about their faith with the family.'

———— o ————

Moore and Diane are based in Belfast, and have three children, Patrick (aged 15), Peter (aged 14) and Sophie (aged 12). Moore and Diane were both brought up in Christian homes, and experienced family devotions from time to time, but it was the example of friends that led them to begin family worship themselves. The family attend a Presbyterian church.

How do we worship together?

The way the family has worshipped together has changed throughout the years. To begin with, it was basic Bible stories and songs, but the family has experimented with all sorts of things through the years – including craft activities and prayer cards, using a basic catechism, and reading through children's Bibles. Nowadays, they have a basic evening pattern, where they meet together after the evening meal, read a Bible passage, and spend time discussing it;

'We tend to work through books of the Bible, going through verse by verse. We've become more systematic with them, as they've got older.'

Moore and Diane also found that sharing a Proverb was a good way to start the day as a family.

'We would read a Proverb, say a little about it, and then pray about the day ahead. It was quite a manageable thing to do.'

What's been challenging?

• Keeping the kids engaged.

'The challenge is trying to refresh things so that you're not always doing the same thing or coming back to things that are very familiar to them'

- Not always seeing a difference.

'I think actually one of the biggest reality-checks is when your Bible time finishes and within two minutes they're annoying each other!'

- Applying the Bible at different stages.

'You're still always trying to work out how it applies appropriately at their age.'

What's worked well?

- Encouragement for parents as well as children.

'Teaching God's Word to our children brings blessing to us as well.'

- Helping kids learn to pray naturally.

'Ultimately for me one of the big pluses of doing it from when they're young is that they don't become self-conscious about praying in front of each other.'

- Helping you see how the kids are doing.

'One of the good things is the insight it gives you into where your children are at. There are some times when they seem less tuned in, but then there are other times when they say something which shows that God is at work in their lives.'

Advice for getting started

- Just start!

'Anything is better than nothing. Just start and keep going. Some nights it'll be terrible, and some nights it'll be great,'

- Family worship shows what is important in your family.

'Even if you don't think you're doing it particularly well, what you are saying is, "this matters in our home. This is something that matters to us."'

- Teach passages not just verses.

'When isolated verses aren't in context, it has some benefit but it is much better if they see the bigger picture of a whole passage.'

Conversations at breakfast

'There is a real blessing to be brought up in a Christian home, and we have a responsibility to teach our children to trust the Lord.'

Phil and Ruth live in Buxton, Derbyshire with their three children, Esther (7), Joel (5) and Lydia (1). They are part of a local Anglican church.

How do we worship together?

For Phil and Ruth, breakfast works best for family worship. Over the table, they talk about God together and spend time praying for others. To help their discussion, they've been reading through the book, *Everything A Child Should Know About God*;

> *'This brings up some really interesting things to talk about as a family, like the Trinity, or angels, or the Gospels.'*

For their prayer time, they've put together a book of photos of people to pray for on each day of the week. Everyone takes a turn to pray for those pictured, and the photos mean that all the children – whatever their reading ability – know who it is they're focusing on;

> *'We will then lift the day up to God and pray for situations we face.'*

Phil and Ruth also try to model praying for others through the day.

> *'If we hear some news that needs prayer, we do try and stop and pray about it. The children are also very good at reminding us that we can pray for things.'*

As well as family worship at breakfast time, Phil and Ruth read through the Bible and pray with each of their children at night before bed. Since their children are at different ages, each child has a different kind of Bible. These include picture books and Bible activity books, while they are helping their eldest child, Esther, to read through a Gospel in the NIV.

What's been challenging?

- Discipline.

'I think a challenge is the discipline of making it actually happen, because we don't manage it every day without fail.'

- Tiredness.

'The hardest times have been when we haven't had much sleep, and the mornings have been a bit more muddled as one of us has been trying to catch up on sleep.'

What's worked well?

- Praying together.

'Praying together can take some tension out of the rest of the morning. I know it has brought peace and help to the children's hearts when there are things that they are concerned about that we just can't fix.'

- Admitting sin.

'There are times we need to confess sin to God but also to the kids, so at night-time we say a sorry prayer to God alongside the children and admit that we are not always right.'

- Encouraging the children to pray.

'We learn from the children's prayers, from their heart for the non-Christians that they know, and are encouraged and challenged by their simple faith.'

Advice for getting started

- Start early.

'A big tip would be to start young, as soon as you would sit with your child on your knee to read a book.'

- Talking to others.

'I think talking to others and asking what they are doing and what they are using is a help.'

- Think about the whole of life.

'I think it's also about sharing your life and faith with your children as you go throughout the day.'

Discipleship in the family

'In the home, we want to make faith very normal. We just want to try and bring up our sons as disciples of Jesus.'

———•———

Jamie and Kate live in Dromore, County Down with their two children, Toby (aged 3) and Joel (5 months old). Jamie and Kate see their children as members of God's 'covenant people', with family worship helping their kids learn what it means to be followers of Jesus. They are members of the Presbyterian Church.

How do we worship together?

Family worship follows a simple pattern. As they sit down before dinner, Jamie reads a short passage of Scripture, gives a brief explanation of its meaning, and asks one or two questions. The family then pray for one another. They have sought to keep family worship simple so that it's easy to do each day.

Jamie and Kate also encourage Toby to pray at bedtime;

> *'I would ask Toby for three things;*
> *what he wants to say thank you*
> *to Jesus for, what he wants to say*
> *sorry to Jesus for, and what he*
> *wants to ask Jesus' help for.'*

Jamie has also developed a short catechism, a tool for teaching his children truths about God. Rather than working through a set of questions and answers – as many catechisms do – Jamie has put together a set of rhyming verses to make it more memorable for the kids.

> *'We try and do these verses all the time. We're constantly trying*
> *to practise them with Toby.'*

For Jamie and Kate, family worship isn't usually dramatic, and it can be hard work. But they're convinced that it's a way through which God works.

> *'It's not a road to Damascus kind of experience. It's just what we*
> *do. It's trying to build the daily means of grace into Toby and*
> *Joel's life.'*

What's been challenging?

- Finding space and time.

'Even the discipline of sitting down at the table together doesn't always happen. The main challenge is getting space as a family together.'

- Leading worship with young children.

'We have to show a lot of patience at times. Just getting Toby to sit still for 30 seconds is difficult enough!'

What's worked well?

- Keeping it simple.

'If we tried to do a craft activity, we wouldn't do it because we couldn't find the time. Keeping it really simple has enabled us to make it a much more regular practice.'

- Knowing that God speaks.

'Whenever we open Scripture, even if Toby is throwing carrots across the table, God wants to speak to us.'

- Showing that faith is part of the home.

'Faith should be something that's very normal in our home. We want our kids to see us pray and read the Bible, but we also want to teach them to do it and model that for them.'

Advice for getting started

- Just do it!

'Keep it simple and do it! Just go ahead and do it.'

- Accept the chaos with younger children.

'It doesn't matter that there's chaos! They're three and one, and they don't always have to be pious and sit still.'

- Don't give up.

'If you don't do it or you miss a day, just get on and do it the next day. Ignore the idea that you can't come to God because you've not been for so long.'

Faith begins at home

'We are giving our children a spiritual investment. We are preparing them so that they won't leave the Christian faith.'

Irfan and Raheela have four children, Karam (23), Iram (21), Daud (16) and Iraj (12). Originally from Pakistan, the family came to the UK seeking asylum in 2005, and are now based in Cardiff. Irfan and Raheela attend a Methodist Church and grew up in families that worshipped together.

How do we worship together?

The family worship together each evening. After lighting a candle, they spend time in prayer, the singing of (Urdu) Psalms and songs, and reading and discussing a passage – usually a chapter of Scripture. This is a key time for the family, and normally takes place in the family living room.

Irfan and Raheela encourage their children to learn Scripture themselves, including key themes within each book. When the children were younger, they used children's Bibles, but now read through the Bible in Urdu together.

> *'We are praying with our Bibles. We are familiar with them.'*

Music is important during worship, and bongo drums accompany the singing. Irfan and Raheela also sometimes include short 'Bible quizzes' to make the time varied and fun, and all the kids participate in prayer, reading and singing. Memory verses are also dotted throughout the house alongside images from the Bible.

> *'You can see signs that we are Christians. Every second of life you need to remember who you are.'*

Irfan and Raheela believe that family worship is crucial because faith begins at home. It should always be a priority for families to share God's love with one another.

> *'You have to look after your home first.'*

What's been challenging?

- Finding the right time for family worship.

'As our children grew older, the times when we were all together changed, and so when we met for family worship was different.'

What's worked well?

- Encouraging our kids to pray.

'When our children were little, we used to encourage them to pray for the family. Even if they prayed just two or three sentences, that was the prayer for the evening.'

- Taking turns to read the Bible.

'Our children confidently choose one person from the Bible, one passage, or a verse, and tell you about it.'

Advice for getting started

- Find something that works best for your family.

'Every family is different, and every family is going to worship differently.'

- Pray with your children as well as for your children.

'People say, 'we are praying for our children'; try to pray with them too!'

- Make family worship fun.

'It's really important to make it fun and enjoyable, so they learn that God and family worship aren't boring.'

Growing as disciples, together

'We're the ones who are first and foremost responsible for the discipleship of our daughter.'

———— • ————

Darrell, Terri and their daughter, Noel (aged 10), are an American family living in North London and are part of an Anglican church. Darrell and Terri both come from Christian families but family worship was never a central part of their lives growing up. It is something they have come to as a family with Noel.

How do we worship together?

Worshipping together usually takes place over breakfast, but sometimes Darrell's job means that evening works better instead. Either way, food always helps.

> *'We find sitting down round the table, especially over food, is a great time for it.'*

Family worship has changed over the years. When Noel was young, printed Bible cards were helpful in prompting discussion and prayer. In more recent years, Darrell and Terri have used book and website resources to guide what they do at home. Latterly they have been using *Training Hearts, Teaching Minds*, which provides a systematic, question based framework for devotionals. Helping Noel grasp key teachings of the faith is an important part of worshipping together.

> *'Noel gets a chance to ask questions, which is often asking Darrell to use smaller, more simple words!'*

Prayer is always important in family worship, and the family draw on different resources to help them pray for others;

> *'For example we use the Joshua Project (joshuaproject.net) which is a website that helps us see all the people who have not yet been reached with the Christian message'*

What's been challenging?

- A lack of role models.

'We feel that one of the biggest challenges is that we never had this modelled for us as we grew up so we feel like we're making it up as we go along.'

- Family worship is counter-cultural.

'It's simply not something that is a part of British church culture and it always takes effort to be counter-cultural.'

- We don't always know the answers!

'There is loads of stuff we don't know and sometimes we have to say that to Noel.'

What's worked well?

- Growing as a family in faith.

'We've been blessed because we get to talk to each other about Jesus and see each other's faith grow.'

- Preparing for the future.

'We won't see the full fruit of what we're doing for many years, but it's essential preparation for the years to come for all of us.'

- Inspiring other families.

'We've also seen what we do as a blessing to other families as Noel is able to help other children as they ask questions which we've covered in our times together.'

Advice for getting started

- Just start.

'Just start something, take a step and do something that points your child to Jesus.'

- Plan to worship together.

'We plan everything else in life so we should definitely plan family worship. If we don't protect it and prioritise it, then life will simply take over.'

Keeping Jesus as the centre

'We wanted to bring Jesus into the centre of our family, into the centre of who we are and what we do.'

———— ● ————

Celeste and Tim live in North London with their two daughters, Keziah (aged 10) and Beulah (aged 6). They attend an Anglican church and began to worship together as a family, more intentionally, a year and a half ago.

How do we worship together?

The family worships together in the evenings. They read together a passage of the Bible, using Bible notes for kids, called XTB. These notes offer questions for the kids and also show the links between Bible passages and Jesus. Jesus is always central.

The family have produced 'glitter cards' to help them pray, which Keziah and Beulah helped to make.

> *'We write names of friends, family and other people we want to pray for and also topics such as a global issue in the news; it helps keep our prayer time short and focused.'*

The cards sit in a decorated jewellery box, and different cards are used each day to pray for others.

They seek to keep Jesus central in every part of life, but recognise that having a 'set time' for praying and reading the Bible together is also important.

> *'We want our children to begin to own the faith for themselves.'*

What's been challenging?

- Busyness of life.

'We have found that the evenings work best for us, but as any parent knows, after school there is homework and all manner of clubs and so we have to vary timings and how we approach our time together; for example, sometimes we might use time in the car to talk about God or pray.'

- Keeping Going.

'Sometimes we might only get to spend this time together two or three

times in a week, but we don't let that put us off. We reason that something is better than nothing.'

• Children at different stages.
'Our elder daughter is getting a bit old for what we are currently doing so we're thinking about how to change things to adapt to that; we know things can't stay the same. We've started introducing Bible notes for older children, which she is beginning to do on her own.'

• A demanding job.
'Tim can't always be involved as he's not back from work, though if he is back early enough he will try to join in.'

What's worked well?

• Following Jesus as a family.
'It's no longer four individuals who sign up to the Christian faith and who go to church on Sunday, it's shaping and identifying us as a family following Christ.'

• Keeping faith in all of life.
'Our children get to see and hear us talking about faith in the home and car and everyday life.'

• Helping our kids (and us!) talk about faith.
'It felt strange at first but we are getting used to talking about the Bible and how it applies to our lives.'

Advice for getting started

• Just do something.
'Something will be better than nothing, even a short, simple reading, or prayer, or an activity.'

- Encourage kids to talk.

'Try to do something that gets them talking; something that prompts them to ask questions and express their thoughts.'

- Choose what works.

'If they like drawing then draw, if they like craft then make things together.'

- Be patient.

'Getting children involved in reading the Bible and praying (or at least praying sensible prayers!) can take time.

Laying good foundations

'If we give them good foundations, they will build on them.'

———— ● ————

Ade and Funmi live in Glasgow with their four children, Dammy (10), Ayo (8), and their twin girls Korede and Kayode (aged 6). Originally from Nigeria, they moved to the UK in 2009, and now live in Glasgow where they worship at a Pentecostal Church. Ade and Funmi grew up in families that worshipped together, and seek to pass on what they have learnt to their own children.

How do we worship together?

Family worship began from the start for Ade and Funmi. They prayed for the children 'from the womb', and – when their children were able to speak – encouraged them also to talk to God and listen to the Scriptures.

'As soon as they began to speak, we encouraged them to participate.'

Worship now takes place each morning and evening. In the morning, the family begin by singing praises to God – sometimes accompanied with a tambourine.

'We are from a Pentecostal background, and that affects how we worship.'

Prayers follow the songs. These include prayers for God's presence, for God's forgiveness for sins committed, and for particular concerns. An important part of worshipping together over time is to notice and give thanks for all the prayers that are answered, and this builds up trust that God is at work. Each member of the family takes turns to pray, and so the children learn to pray alongside Ade and Funmi.

'Because we pray together, it's like we have a common plan, a common goal.'

The family also read the Bible together and listen to a story, using an online devotional 'Keys for Kids' (www.keysforkids.org). This leads to discussion and conversation about the key point of the story and how it relates to the Bible. Memorising the Bible is also part of worshipping together.

What's been challenging?

- Engaging the kids.

'At the early stage the children didn't like it, but now they ask us to do it.'

What's worked well?

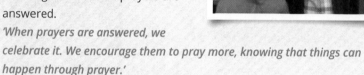

- Creating a habit.

'Even if we're not around, they know to start the day with worship.'

- Giving thanks when prayers are answered.

'When prayers are answered, we celebrate it. We encourage them to pray more, knowing that things can happen through prayer.'

- Praying throughout the day.

'We have given them the culture to pray over whatever they eat and drink.'

Advice for getting started

- Start early.

'The best way is to start as early as possible.'

- It won't always be easy.

'No matter how soon you start, there will be challenges from children, but the more you explain it to them, the more they will appreciate it.'

- Use stories.

'Most children like to hear a story before they go to bed, and so you can begin by using stories when starting family worship.'

Learning from our children

'We are discovering things with them by asking questions.'

Originally from Hungary, Kata and Tibor now live in Reading with their twin 5 year old girls, Zsofi and Tami. Kata and Tibor belong to a local independent evangelical church, which has encouraged them to nurture faith at home.

How do we worship together?

Kata and Tibor seek to worship together with their children through praying and reading Scripture together each evening. While prayer happens every night, they also seek to read the Bible regularly to their girls and discuss the passage using *The Beginner's Bible* and a resource called, *Beginning with God*.

> *'Prayer is always there, but the ideal would be to use the Bible and a Bible resource each day too.'*

They also encourage their children to pray together over meals, with Zsofi and Tami often reciting set prayers.

> *'We prayed even when they were babies... Each day a different person prays at mealtime, and this has really encouraged them to pray.'*

Kata and Tibor are particularly encouraged by the church they attend to worship together within the family, and feel that faith is reinforced across the board for their daughters through the range of their relationships.

What's been challenging?

- Finding time to pray.

'Struggling with time is the biggest challenge.'

- The tiredness of children.

'Now that they've started school, they are really tired. It's a long day, and they're only five years old.'

- Encouraging growth in prayer.

'It goes really well with the things they are thankful for, but they don't mention anything that they are sorry for... I'm struggling with that.'

What's worked well?

- Learning from the faith of children.

'Their faith is strong, so definitely we can learn from that. They love God.'

- Helping the children process the day in prayer.

'It's evening, and it's quiet, and with the prayer you're processing the day. It's a nice end to the day; they know that our last sentence is a prayer.'

- Demonstrating forgiveness.

'It's just good to go in front of God and show them that maybe I was a bit cross with Daddy or with them but we can resolve it.'

Advice for getting started

- Trust God for your children's faith.

'Our children's faith is not fully dependent on us. It's a big relief; we can only do so much.'

- Encourage children in church.

'The church is so important. One of our daughter's friends is so passionate about Jesus, and we can hear her encouraging our children.'

- Live out your faith in all of life.

'Spend time living out your worship during the day. Speak and talk about God and ask questions.'

Liturgy for children

'Children are such liturgical beings;
things happen because there are habits.'

———— o ————

Sam and Sara live in Luton with their daughter, Ella (aged 8)
and their son, Theo (aged 5). They worship at a Baptist church
and have also set up a simple service at their home for
parents and children.

How do we worship together?

Family worship started with simply reading an evening Bible story together, which Sam and Sara began when their daughter was young. They've used a range of Bibles, finding that variety has been helpful, but *The Lion Children's Bible* has been a particular favourite.

In more recent years, Sam and Sara have developed a basic 'liturgy' – a simple form of worship – to use at home. The liturgy follows the Bible reading, and is structured around the 'ACTS' prayer; Adoration, Confession, Thanksgiving and Supplication.

'The adoration is usually a song which they choose; and then we tend to lump confession and thanksgiving together; and then the supplication is if there is anything to pray for.'

The liturgy ends with an evening song that Sam and his daughter wrote, and which has now become part of the worship time. The song includes a prayer against bad dreams, for a good night's sleep, and for God's protection.

For the family, keeping it simple has been important. Having a routine means that family worship is a habit at home, a way of ensuring that the children learn to pray and trust God.

'They do things because we've always done them and they want to do them the same way. Normally they're not interested in newfangled ways of doing things.'

Sam and Sara also encourage their children to worship God outside and in the everyday, as well as during play. This helps break down any sense that there is a barrier between worship and normal life, and is a reminder that God can be worshipped in every circumstance.

What's been challenging?

- The kids aren't always interested.

'Some of the struggle is that the children don't always want to do it!'

- Engaging with the children.

'The challenge is meeting them where they are and finding ways of engaging them.'

- It's not always easy.

'I need to be okay with the fact that they wrestled all the way through that prayer time.'

What's worked well?

- Regular Bible reading.

'When they were small we were getting nowhere with the Bible reading, but now I realise that the trickle effect of doing it pretty much every night is that they know all the key Bible stories.'

- A time to share.

'It's helpful that we have an outlet for talking about things that are scary and things that are worrying.'

- Creating the right atmosphere.

'They are picking up whether what we do is welcoming, and forgiving, and loving.'

Advice for getting started

- Keep going.

'When they're pre-school, you don't have to feel like you're getting somewhere – just the fact that you're doing it is almost enough of what they need for that age.'

- Find out what works for your family.

'Our family does music, but that's not the case in every family. It's important to find what you already do and work worship into that.'

- Don't leave it to the experts.

'You don't have to be an expert. The expert doesn't know your children. Have the confidence that your faith is worth communicating.'

The comfort of catechesis

TWO BOYS (AGED 3 & 1), CAMBRIDGE

'Don't get caught up in the idea that catechism is a heavy-handed, scary concept for kids. It's really not; it's just instruction.

———— • ————

Originally from America, William and Kelli live in Cambridge with their two sons, Amos (aged 3) and Lucas (aged 1). They have spent much of the last year in California where their eldest son Amos had a tumour removed after an overnight diagnosis of brain cancer. Amos' recovery continues, and William and Kelli testify to the way in which worshipping together at home has helped to sustain them throughout the past year. The family belong to the Presbyterian Church.

How do we worship together?

Family worship has always involved reading through the Bible together, and William and Kelli have found *The Jesus Storybook Bible* a wonderful resource to spark discussion with the kids. William and Kelli also encourage the children to learn memory verses, which often takes place in the midst of play during the day.

As well as reading the Bible together, the family have in recent years begun using the *First Catechism*, 150 questions and answers that help children learn about the Christian faith. Prior to the discovery of his tumour, Amos had learned about 30 questions.

> *'With Amos, we started when he was two and a half, and we made it part of his bedtime routine. Amos really took to them, and basically we will read a question and answer and ask Amos to repeat the answer. Amos was always very excited when he got to add a new question.'*

Following the catechism, the family pray together, often incorporating the catechism answer into the prayer itself. The catechism and children's Bible are a great combination, helping the kids to learn the story of God as well as key beliefs about God.

The last six months has seen a huge change for the family. Following Amos' brain surgery, there has been a lengthy recovery in hospital and ongoing rehabilitation. But even at the times when Amos could neither move nor talk, William and Kelli knew God's presence.

> *'Knowing what Amos knew about the Lord was invaluable to us because we could use the questions that he knew to pray out the catechism and remind him that the Lord made him and takes care of him, for his own glory.'*

Five months after the surgery, as Amos' speech and movement began to return, William and Kelli were amazed to find that Amos remembered 28 of the 30 catechism questions he had learned. A key memory verse for the family remains Psalm 144:5; *'Happy are those whose God is the Lord!'*

What's worked well?

• Simplicity of Use.
'The thing that we really like about the catechism is that it's organised for you. It takes a lot of the leg work out of the equation and makes family worship and instruction of the children in the Lord actually a lot easier.'

• Working with the way kids learn.
'Rote learning through the catechism sounds really negative, but that's what little kids do to learn; they just repeat things. It's their whole mode of learning.'

• Giving kids key concepts.
'It's giving your kids raw material, conceptual raw material, to learn with.'

What's been challenging?

• Consistency.
'I think no matter what sort of family worship you're doing, the biggest challenge is just being consistent. You have to sit down and do it with your kids.'

• It can be hard work.
'It takes effort. It's a task that we have to put our hands to.'

• Working with different ages.
'One of the things that has been challenging is trying to figure out how to do family worship in a way that makes sense for both boys.'

Advice for getting started

- It's never too late.

'It's never too late to start. I'm not getting anything more right than you for having started with younger kids.'

- Start slowly.

'It's something you want to ease into. Pick something that is natural for your family and start from there.'

- Model loving God throughout the day.

'Kids love what you love, and so it's worth it for your kids to hear you talking about God all the time and experience that sort of environment.'

Through the Bible, book by book

TWO BOYS (AGED 11 & 5), LANCASTER

'We wanted to bring Jesus into the centre of our family.'

———— • ————

Andy and Jo live in Lancaster with their two sons, Daniel (aged 11) and Matthew (aged 5). They are members of an Evangelical Free Church where they have been consistently encouraged to disciple their children by teaching them the Bible.

How do we worship together?

After trying various resources, Andy and Jo decided to write their own materials for their eldest son, Daniel, when he was 7, aiming to go book by book through the Bible.

> *'Other stuff didn't seem to work for us, so we just started reading Matthew's Gospel with a few questions of our own to get us started and it worked well.'*

Because Andy's job means he leaves the house very early, he prepares questions on each passage and Jo leads the devotions over breakfast in the morning. The questions are aimed at Daniel, but Matthew is always there and is growing into it.

> *'Matthew's never known anything different; it's just natural for him for us to study the Bible together as a family.'*

Andy and Jo have also felt that reading together through the Gospels has been particularly important. They are great for provoking questions and discussion.

> *'The Gospels take us straight to the person and work of Jesus and are accessible, compelling narratives.'*

Although Andy is not normally there, he is part of family devotions through writing the materials and is able to look over Daniel's answers in the evening.

> *'I've been able to be involved and direct what Daniel is doing through deciding which books of the Bible to do and writing the materials in advance.'*

What's been challenging?

- Time consuming.

'Writing our own materials, including overviews of each book, questions, and activities is really effective, but it takes a lot of time.'

- Being creative and keeping it fresh.

'The materials sometimes feel a bit academic. It's not been a problem for Daniel, but as Matthew joins in more, we may need to adapt things and be more creative.'

- Getting beyond the head to the heart.

'It's good to study the Bible but what we really want is for our children not merely to know about God, but to know God personally through Jesus.'

What's worked well?

- Managing the challenge of long working days.

'Through writing the materials, I've been able to lead the devotions and share in them in some way even though I'm not able to be there most days.'

- Participation not supervision.

'The way we've worked it means that we don't feel we're supervising a child's activity but studying the Bible together.'

- Encouraging others.

'We've been able to show other parents at church what we do and show them that they could try something similar.'

- Talking about faith.

'Having a regular time together means that talking about faith is normal for us. It has also helped us talk along the way about how things are going in school, church or with their friends.'

Advice for getting started

- Be child specific.

'Be intentional in considering what works for your child given their character and personality.'

- Make it a whole family thing.

'Watch out you don't fall into the trap of simply supervising a children's activity; aim for a time together with God.'

- Consider your legacy.

'Think about when your children are 18 and you look back over your time with them, what do you want to see? It might be hard work but if you want them to follow Jesus at 18 then doing something like this together is crucial.'

Questions, answers and enquiring minds

'If faith comes through hearing, then tell your children the good news of Jesus, and let them tell you the good news too, and faith in God in your home will grow.'

———•———

Jonathan and Joanna live in Mold with their two daughters, Izabella (aged 4) and Natalia (aged 2). Jonathan is Welsh and Joanna is Polish; they are members of a Baptist Church in North Wales.

How do we worship together?

For the last year and a half, Jonathan and Joanna have had a short devotional time with their two daughters over breakfast.

'We do it at breakfast because it's when the girls are at their best in terms of being attentive and engaged. Because it's first thing they're not tired, and being at the table also helps them focus on our time together.'

They are currently using *Everything a child should know about God* which works through questions of faith systematically.

'We like the book we're using now because it provides a structured approach which brings up topics you might not otherwise talk about like who is the Holy Spirit and what are angels; it has good pictures and gives great questions which help us discuss the topic with Izabella and Natalia.'

Prayer and singing follow on naturally.

'We then pray a simple prayer related to the questions we've looked at that shows the girls they can pray too, which Izabella is starting to do. We sometimes turn our prayers into songs using familiar nursery rhymes but change the words. We also write prayers down in books we have for each of them, books that capture all sorts of things about their life, including what God has done.'

Morning worship, however, is not the end of the story.

'When we're out and about, we always look for opportunities

to talk about God. Maybe when we're in the park and they ask why the leaves fall from the trees, we take the opportunity to say something about God's amazing creation.'

What's been challenging?

• The busyness of life!
'We both work so fitting it in can sometimes be difficult. At least twice a week we won't get round to it.'

• Sleep deprivation.
'Our girls are still quite young and we don't get as much sleep as we would like and that makes the mornings difficult. It's a lot better now, but even still, tiredness is a challenge for us.'

What's worked well?

• Provoking questions.
'The systematic approach provokes all sorts of great questions from our girls; when we studied the Trinity and the person of Jesus, Izabella asked: 'Why is Jesus praying to himself?''

• Giving them confident enquiring minds.
'We want them to see that they can ask any questions they want and they won't be brushed off with a trite answer. We'll talk through good answers to their great questions; this means they not only see that there are good answers, but they get used to thinking these things through.'

• Getting to know each other better.
'When we sit around God's Word we glorify him and it brings us closer as a family. We get to know each other better so when we pray we can pray knowing what is important to each of us individually.'

- Learning from them.

'We've learnt from them because their approach to faith is so open and bold. They discover things and then act on what they know; it's a great reminder of what adults often get wrong.'

Advice for getting started

- Be encouraged.

'Don't go into it just expecting it to be a burden as you'll be encouraged over time by their growth and reactions. When you're encouraged you'll want to do more. There are discouragements, but the rewards outweigh them.'

- Balance structure with flexibility.

'Having a deliberately structured, regular time together is vital as children thrive on that, but day to day be ready to alter what you do depending on how they react.'

Worshipping at the table

'If our faith is the basis of our relationship,
it's got to be the basis of our family.'

———— • ————

Marina and Grant live in Mortimer, near Reading, and have three
children, Michali (14), Asher (11) and Demi (9). Marina and Grant
are originally from South Africa, while Marina also comes from a
Jewish background and this shapes how the family worship together.
The family attends a local independent evangelical church.

How do we worship together?

The family worships together around the table over a weekly 'Shabbat' meal, where they talk and pray over bread and wine (and juice for the kids). The Shabbat meal follows a main family meal, and usually takes place on a Friday or Saturday night.

As well as praying traditional Hebrew prayers, and acknowledging Jesus as the Messiah, the family light a candle together and thank the Lord for being the light of the world.

'We always start by giving thanks. Everyone needs to think from their week what they want to thank God for, and we pray together as a family.'

Grant and Marina also read a short passage of Scripture. They find that talking about faith together over a meal is a great place for exploring questions of faith, and also seems to reflect the way in which Jesus ministered.

Bedtimes are always a time of prayer, where issues that emerge during the day are brought to God. The family also listens to worship CDs during regular car journeys, and find that such journeys can also be times of prayer,

'We're in the car a lot, and a lot of prayer happens.'

What's been challenging?

- Tiredness.

'Sometimes we tire. We have to make the effort and sometimes we don't feel like it.'

- Staying focused on God.

'I think definitely it's the thing of discipline, but closing our eyes in prayer helps us focus.'

- Finding time.

'It's getting to the point where there is so much going on with the kids that we have to just stop and make the time – we will never get it back!'

What's worked well?

- Keeping it short.

'We don't read long chapters; we just choose a verse or a Psalm.'

- Making sure it's fun.

'We decided to make it short and enjoyable. It's always got an enjoyable memory and feeling about it.'

- Asking lots of questions.

'We ask questions, things come up; they know it's a safe environment.'

Advice for getting started

- Family worship helps kids learn about faith.

'Our number one thing is that they come to a full understanding of what it means to be a Christian; everything hangs on that.'

- Bring worship into the whole of life.

'My favourite verse is, 'I will never leave you, nor forsake you.' We bring the Lord into our everyday'

- Worshipping around food can be great!

'I'd say, worship together around a table over a meal. Such a special thing happens when you're eating together.'

'We plan everything else in life, so we should definitely plan family worship. If we don't protect it and prioritise it, then life will simply take over.'

Conclusion

FAMILY WORSHIP IN YOUR HOME

As for me and my household, we will serve the Lord'.
Joshua 24:15b

Whether you are starting family worship for the first time or have been doing it for a while, the 15 stories in *Together with God* can give you ideas to draw on as you think about what will work best in your own home.

In this final chapter, we will offer *advice for parents wishing to start family worship*. Our recommendations echo the tips given by many of the families in this book, so think of this section as a summary of what's been shared. We will also address key *questions about family worship*, touching on issues such as the role of grandparents and how church leaders can help families worship together.

The bulk of this chapter is a guide to *recommended resources*. As well as including those mentioned by the families we have interviewed, we will signpost a range of other resources for beginning family worship.

In a 'final word', we offer you some reflections on the *joy of family worship*. Joy may seem a peculiar adjective to use for something that is at times hard work, but we are convinced that families come to know the joy and love of Christ more deeply as they worship together.

STARTING FAMILY WORSHIP

If you're starting family worship for the first time, consider following these six steps that we've drawn from the advice families have shared.

1. Pray for God's Help

Apart from God's grace, nothing is possible in the Christian life – and that's true of family worship as much as anything else. Ask God to help you as you begin to explore worshipping together at home. Seek His wisdom to know what will work best for your family.

Make sure too that you don't neglect your own time with God. As we spend time growing in the grace of God – in prayer and with Scripture – so too we can help our children discover that same grace.

2. Choose your time and place

Think carefully about what is realistic for you as a parent but also what works best with your children. When are they most alert? When are they least busy? Do you need to limit the number of after-school clubs to make room for family worship?

Think too about how frequently you'd like to worship together as a family. Many families choose to meet daily for worship, but you might find that a weekly commitment suits your family best.

Reflect too on the best place for family worship, which may depend on where you have the best conversations with your children. Some families meet over the dining table, while others gather in the lounge or in a child's bedroom.

3. Keep it simple

At its simplest, family worship involves praying and reading the Bible together. If you don't pray together as a family, you might start by saying grace together at meal times. Once that's an established habit, you could choose a passage of Scripture to read and discuss as the meal ends. Or it may be that praying with your child and reading a Bible story at bedtime works best. Don't overcomplicate the early stages of family worship; do what's realistic and simple.

The list of resources provided in this chapter can also give you some ideas and structures for daily or weekly worship times. If they are part of your church tradition, Advent or Lent can also provide good opportunities for beginning family worship.

4. Do something that suits your children

Are your children creative, musical, sporty or academic (or all of the above)? Are they shy or confident? Go with something which suits your children's character and temperament. If you feel they would react well, ask them what they would like to do for family worship. Think about the stories in *Together with God*, and about what you could adapt from other families for your own home.

Focusing on what might suit your children won't mean that they will automatically love what you have prepared. All the families we interviewed shared times when it was hard-going, and when children didn't connect. Finding ways of worship that suit your family, however, will make getting through these times easier.

5. Tell someone

Tell someone in your church about what you're planning; ask them to pray for you and follow up with you on how it's going after a few weeks.

By sharing your story and your struggle with others, you might also be an encouragement for other families to begin family worship in their own homes. Many of the families we interviewed began family worship because their friends modelled it with their own families, and you could do the same for others as well.

6. Keep going

Family worship isn't always easy, so don't be put off by difficulties. Ask God for his strength to keep going and commit to it for the long haul.

Remember that every family goes through periods when family worship, for whatever reason, drops off the radar. But it's never too late to begin again, so don't let failure stop you re-starting. Stay the course!

QUESTIONS ABOUT FAMILY WORSHIP

The following questions emerged from conversations with our interviewees and others about family worship.

• How do I find time for family worship?

Time can seem to be in short supply, and – in families where both parents are working – it can be difficult for families to meet together. We tend to find time for what is important to us, and making time for family worship may mean sacrificing other commitments (perhaps giving up a TV show).

Aim to start small. Something small and regular is better than something lengthy and infrequent. Remember that family worship is a way of living out faith in the home, as well as opening up as a family to God's grace.

• How can I lead family worship if my spouse isn't a Christian?

Christians who are married to non-Christians can find it hard to know what to do about family worship. Begin with talking to your spouse about your desire to share your faith with your children, even if it's just an evening Bible story and prayer before bed. If your husband or wife is uncomfortable with this, pray for opportunities to live out your faith in the home in other ways.

The Bible teaches that God can bless families through the believing parent (1 Cor 7:12-14), and Christian spouses and parents are called to pray for their husbands or wives and for their children. In the New Testament, Timothy's Christian mother shaped his faith (Acts 16:1; 2 Tim 1:5; 3:15), while the later church leader Augustine credited his conversion to his mother's prayers. Don't underestimate your impact within the home, even if it's sometimes hard to see.

For some helpful general guidance on marriage when one parent isn't a Christian, see Lee Strobel, *Surviving a Spiritual Mismatch in Marriage* (Grand Rapids, Michigan: Zondervan, 2002).

• How can I lead family worship as a single parent?

Raising children raises challenges at the best of times, and single parents have all the responsibilities but not all the help that couples have.

Finding time may be more difficult, but remember that God will work in your family as you worship together. Try to find a way of worshipping that fits your family's unique shape.

• Shouldn't my children come to their own decision about faith?

Some parents fear that family worship might risk 'indoctrinating' their child or children, and wonder whether they should leave their kids to make up their own minds about faith when they are older. But all parents – whether Christians, atheists, or adherents of a different religion – bring children up with a set of beliefs, practices and values. As Christian parents, our calling is to help our children know what it means to worship God (Father, Son and Spirit) and live for Him (Deut 6:4-9; Eph 6:4).

Research also shows that parents who model their faith within the home give their children the best chance of discovering faith for themselves.[21] Worshipping together within the home is a key part of this, and can help children trust and love God for themselves.

• As a grandparent, how can I be involved?

If you are a grandparent, consider building elements of family worship into the time you spend with your grandchild or grand-children. This might include reading a Bible story, praying together, or spending time at church. If your children are Christian, you will be reinforcing the faith taught in the home. If your children aren't Christians, they may still value your contribution in the lives of their children. Talk with them if you aren't sure, and try to make faith and worship a natural part of the time you spend with your grandkids.

Research also shows that the influence of grandparents on the faith of their grandchildren is more significant than many realise.[22] Grandparents are key Christian role models for their grandchildren, and can share through their life and words how faith in Christ makes a difference.

• As a church leader, how can I encourage family worship within the church?

In our experience, family worship is seldom addressed by ministers or church leaders – although we know that there are some significant exceptions! If you are a church leader and haven't ever taught on this area, consider addressing it within a sermon at some stage, perhaps preaching on one of the texts mentioned in our introduction.

One of the key roles of a youth or children's worker can be to help the older generations to be involved with the faith of the youngest members of the church, whether they are related to them or not. Youth and children's workers are also well placed to promote family worship as they talk with parents about their children.

We also think it's a great idea to share stories about family worship within the church. Consider asking one or two families who practise family worship to share what they do with others. You could also put on display different resources for family worship, and perhaps present *Together with God* as a gift to families who bring a child for baptism or a dedication.

• I didn't lead family worship with my kids and they've left the faith. What can I do?

Some parents reading this may have older children who have left the faith. This is troubling for any parent, and can lead to a sense of guilt and shame. Parents can feel that they could have – and should have – done more, and may regret the absence of family worship when their kids were younger.

If this is the case for you, be honest with God about your feelings, and perhaps pray about it with some Christian friends. Every parent fails in all sorts of ways, but God's forgiveness is constant (Lam 3:22-23). Remember that God loves your children even more than you do, and continue to pray for them.

Your impact on your children continues through life, and research shows that some who leave the faith when they are young will return to it at a later stage of life.[23] Make sure you keep an 'open door' to your children, and show acceptance and love to them even if you feel hurt over the choices they have made.

For a helpful book in this area, see Jo Swinney and Katharine Hill, *Keeping faith… Being family when belief is in question* (Scripture Union, 2012). For a powerful and hopeful story of leaving faith and finding it again, see Gavin Calver, *Disappointed with Jesus: Why do so many young people give up on God?* revised and updated (Oxford: Monarch Books, 2010).

• **Does family worship mean that my kids will definitely be Christians when they're older?**

Unsurprisingly, nothing can 'guarantee' our children will remain or become Christians. If we accept that faith is a gift of God, and so always remains somewhat mysterious, we also have to accept that the home we provide can't 'make' our children trust and follow Christ.

What family worship does do, however, is to model the importance of faith within the home, and so gives children the best chance of making it their own. Sociologists have found that the children of families that worship together are far more likely to remain Christians when they're older, while sending children to Sunday school without helping kids grow in the faith at home has far less effect on a child's future faith.[24]

Whatever paths our children later take, family worship is part of our calling as Christian parents (or a Christian parent). It is only God that can give our children life, but we can pray that God's Spirit will work through our efforts to worship together at home.

RECOMMENDED RESOURCES

The following lists represent our recommendations for starting family worship. We include all the resources mentioned in the stories of family worship, as well as other resources that we would recommend. This is not an exhaustive list, but we hope it will give you a good place to start as you explore what family worship might look like in your own home.

RESOURCES ON CHRISTIAN PARENTING

Benton, Ann, *Aren't They Lovely When They're Asleep – Lessons in Unsentimental Parenting.* Ross-shire: Christian Focus, 2004.

Chester, Tim and Ed Moll, *Gospel-Centered Family: Becoming the Parents God Wants You To Be.* New Maldon: The Good Book Company, 2010.

Lee, Nicky & Sila, *The Parenting Book.* London: Alpha International, 2009.

Melluish, Mark & Lindsay, *Parenting Children: Making the Most of the Years.* Kingsway, 2007.

Stafford, Tim, *Never Mind the Joneses – Building Christian Values in Your Family.* Milton Keynes: Authentic Media, 2004.

Turner, Rachel, *Parenting Children for a Life of Faith: Helping children meet and know God.* Abingdon: The Bible Reading Fellowship, 2007.

INTRODUCTIONS TO FAMILY WORSHIP

Carr, Francois, *Lead your family in worship – Discovering the Enjoyment of God.* Leominster: Day One Publications, 2008.

Helopoulos, Jason *A Neglected Grace: Family Worship in the Christian Home.* Glasgow: Christian Focus, 2013.

Houser, Jason, Bobby Harrington and Chad Harrington, *Dedicated: Training your Children to Trust and Follow Jesus.* Grand Rapids, Michigan: Zondervan, 2015.

Whitney, Donald *Family Worship.* Illinois: Crossway, 2016.

CHILDREN'S BIBLES AND STORYBOOK BIBLES

The International Children's Bible,
Milton Keynes: Authentic Media, 1991.

Alexander, Pat, *The Lion Children's Bible.*
Oxford: Lion Hudson, 1991.

DeVries, Catherine, *The Beginners Bible.*
Oxford: Lion Hudson, 2005.

Hartman, Bob, *The Lion Storyteller Bible.*
Oxford: Lion Hudson, 2008.

Helm, David, R, *The Big Picture Storybook Bible.*
Illinois: Crossway, 2014.

Lloyd-Jones, Sally, *The Jesus Storybook Bible.*
Grand Rapids, MI: Zondervan, 2007.

Payne, Martyn, and Jane Butcher, *The Barnabas Family Bible – 110 Bible stories for Families to share.* Abingdon: Bible Reading Fellowship, 2014.

GENERAL RESOURCES FOR FAMILY WORSHIP

Bentley-Taylor, Suzie, and Moore, Bekah, *Bake Through the Bible.* New Maldon: The Good Book Company, 2013.

Brannigan, Andrew, *Family Time – 82 Devotional life lessons and simple prayers.* Ross-shire: Christian Focus, 2015.

Buckley, Alice, *Play Through the Bible.* New Maldon: The Good Book Company, 2014.

Helm, David, *The Big Picture Family Devotional,* Illinois: Crossway, 2014.

Lloyd-Jones, Sally, *Thoughts to Make Your Hearts Sing.* Grand Rapids, MI: Zondervan, 2007.

Machowski, Marty, *Long Story Short – Ten-Minute Devotions to Draw Your Family to God.* Greensboro: New Growth Press, 2010.

Mitchell, Alison, *Table Talk – Bible Discovery for Families.* Epsom: The Good Book Company.

Mitchell, Alison, *XTB: Bible Discovery for Children.* Epsom: The Good Book Company.

Taylor, Kenneth, *Everything a Child Should Know About God,* Leyland: 10Publishing, 2014.

Wetham, Jo Boddam, and Alison Mitchell, *Beginning with God* Epsom: The Good Book Company.

CATECHISM RESOURCES FOR FAMILY WORSHIP

Conway, Andrew, *The Shorter Catechism Made Simple.* Greenville, SC: Ambassador Books, 2015.

Ferguson, Sinclair, B, *The Big Book of Questions and Answers – A Family Devotional Guide to the Christian Faith.* Ross-shire: Christian Focus, 1997.

Meade, Star, *Training Hearts, Teaching Minds: Devotions Based on the Shorter Catechism.* Phillipsburg, NJ: P&R Publishing, 2000.

Machowski, Mary and Andy McGuire, *The Ology – Ancient Truths Ever New.* Greensboro: New Growth Press, 2015.

Orthodox Presbyterian Church, *First Catechism: Teaching Children Bible Truths.* Suwanee, GA: Great Commission Publications, 2003.

SEASONAL RESOURCES FOR FAMILY WORSHIP

Bentley-Taylor, Susie, and Bekah Moore, *Bake through the Bible at Christmas,* Epsom: The Good Book Company, 2015.

Butcher, Jane, *Family Fun for Easter – 30 Lent and Easter activities for families to share,* Abingdon: BRF 2011.

Butcher, Jane, *Family Fun for Christmas – 30 holiday activities for families to share,* Abingdon: BRF, 2012.

Butcher, Jane, *Family Fun for Summer – 30 holiday activities for families to share,* Abingdon: BRF, 2012.

Hargreaves, Sam & Sara, *Engage with God Advent Family Creative Journal,* Kent: engageworship.org, 2014.

James, Scott, *Mission Accomplished – A two-week Family Easter Devotional,* Greensboro: New Growth Press, 2015.

Machowski, Marty, *Prepare Him Room: Family Devotional – Celebrating the Birth of Jesus,* Greensboro: New Growth Press, 2014.

WEBSITES THAT AID FAMILY WORSHIP

www.seedsfamilyworship.com
Seeds Family Worship produce songs and CDs based on the Bible. They also provide chord charts and memory cards to help children learn memory verses through music.

www.careforthefamily.org.uk
Care for the family seeks to strengthen family life, and includes a helpful section on 'faith in the family' specifically for Christian parents. A 'Faith in the Family Teaching Pack' provides helpful resources (on DVD) from a conference in 2015.

www.engageworship.org
Engage Worship provides resources for creative worship, including for worship within the home.

www.keysforkids.org
Keys for Kids is an international Christian ministry that provides media resources for families and their children, including a daily devotional.

www.faithinhomes.org.uk
Faith in Homes provides resources and ideas to help families live out Christian faith in the home, as well as researching ways to support faith in families.

www.godforkidsapp.com
A helpful Bible-based App that can teach younger (primary-school) children about God.

www.thejoshuaproject.net

The *Joshua Project* is a resource that helps Christians pray for ethnic people groups around the world with the fewest followers of Christ.

www.newcitycatechism.com

Developed by Timothy Keller and Sam Shammas, the *New City Catechism* is a joint adult and children's catechism with 52 questions and answers. It can also be downloaded as an app, with each question accompanied by a memory verse, commentary, a video and a prayer.

THE JOY OF FAMILY WORSHIP

If you keep my commands, you will remain in my love, just as I have kept my Father's commands and remain in his love. I have told you this so that my joy may be in you and that your joy may be complete. (John 15:10-11)

While family worship may at times seem a burden or a difficult challenge, we're convinced it's also a means to greater and deeper joy in Christ.

This joy doesn't mean – in our experience, at least – that worshipping together is always filled with fun and excitement. Tiredness and agitated kids make it difficult, and a regular routine of family worship can be hard to maintain in the midst of busy lives.

Family worship is also pretty ordinary. The regular practice of praying together and opening Scripture doesn't always lead to a dramatic encounter with God, or even a palpable sense of the Spirit.

Family worship, however, is a way through which God's grace grows. By sowing the seeds of times together with God, families are drawn closer to Christ and to one another – and so deepen their joy in God.

In Jesus' parable of the treasure in the field (Matt 13:44), it is the joy of finding the treasure that leads the man to give up all he has for its sake. The treasure of the kingdom requires sacrifice, but it's a sacrifice born of joy.

In a different context, the apostle Paul writes of the joy the Thessalonians experienced as they heard and received the gospel (1 Thess 1:6). Paul also sees joy as a gift of the Spirit (Gal 5:22), a fruit for which we can pray.

Jesus himself also speaks of the joy he wishes to give his followers, and explains that such joy will come through 'remaining in him' (John 15:1-17). Remaining in Jesus comes through hearing and obeying his Word (John 15:5, 7) and praying – through Jesus – to the Father (John 15:7). As families hear God's Word and speak to God, so they too abide more deeply in Christ and know the joy he has promised.

Our prayer is that you will use this book to help you discover – or rediscover – family worship, so that you will know more deeply the Spirit's joy in your family and your home.

End notes

[1] The research, carried out by Linda Woodhead via a YouGov Poll, shows that 40% of those raised with a Christian upbringing lose their Christian identity, and that 'no religion is the new norm'. For a summary, see **www.technology.org/2016/01/19/why-no-religion-is-the-new-religion** (accessed 15th January 2016). For the broader picture of church decline, including the decline of its youth, see Parker (et al.), *British Social Attitudes 28,* pp. 173-184.

[2] Graham Stanton notes that families are often a 'forgotten factor' within youth ministry but it is families that have the biggest impact on the faith of young people; Stanton, *Families – a Forgotten Factor?* For a demonstration of the importance of parents in passing on the faith, see Bengston, *Families and Faith*

[3] See *The Church Growth Research Programme Report on Strands 1 and 2,* by Voas and Watt (Feb 2014), p. 18. Of 500 Anglican parents surveyed, only 11% saw this as a priority – compared to 94% who identified a key priority as 'good manners' and 83% who pointed to 'tolerance and respect'. Even among those Anglicans who identified religion as 'very important' in their lives, only 36% saw passing on faith as a priority. The full report can be found at **www.churchgrowthresearch.org.uk/UserFiles/File/Reports/Report_Strands_1_2_rev2.pdf**

[4] See the Evangelical Alliance, *21st Century Evangelicals*, pp. 12-13.

[5] For a description of the different forms of family that exist today, see The Methodist Church, *We are Family*, pp. 8-10.

[6] If you're unsure about the value of the Bible, a good place to start might be with Cooper, *Can I Really Trust the Bible?*, Ovey and Strange, *Confident: Why we can trust the Bible,* or DeYoung, *Taking God at His Word.*

[7] For the role of families in the Bible, see the essays on Old Testament and New in M. and M. Anthony, *A Theology for Family Ministries.* See also the discussion on a 'biblical frame for defining family' in Garland, *Family Ministry*, pp. 92-112.

[8] For the variety of ways in which the Old Testament Law values and includes children, see Lawson, 'Old Testament Teaching on the Family,' pp. 81-85.

[9] For commentary on this passage, as well as references to other key texts, see Melick Jr., 'New Testament Teachings on the Family,' pp. 88-105.

[10] On this theme, see Hellerman, *When the Church Was a Family.*

[11] This seems to be the best way of understanding Paul's explanation that the unbelieving husband or wife is 'sanctified' through their spouse, and so their children are 'holy' (1 Cor 7:14).

[12] For a brief survey of the historical practice that informs the summary below, see Jones and Stinson, *Family Ministry Models*, pp. 155-180. For various essays on family discipleship in Christian history, see 'part two' of Jones and Stinson (eds.), *Trained in the Fear of God*.

[13] For a discussion of the way in which a range of Christians in the early church encouraged parents to shape the faith of their youth, see Bakke, *When Children Became People,* pp. 152-222.

[14] The quotation is taken from Chrysostom's treatise, 'An Address on Vainglory and The Right Way for Parents to Bring Up Their Children' in Max L. W. Laistner, *Christianity and Pagan Culture*, pp. 85-122. For a discussion of Chrysostom's approach to parenthood more broadly, see Gurion, 'The Ecclesial Family', pp. 61-77.

[15] As Jones and Stinson point out, even before the Reformation era there was an increasing concern that parents take greater responsibility for the faith of their children, *Family Ministry Models*, pp 159-160. For approaches to children among the Reformers, see the various essays in Bunge, *The Child in Christian Thought*.

[16] For Luther's short catechism, see **www.bookofconcord.org/smallcatechism.php**

[17] For the Puritan practice of family worship, see Beeke and Jones, *A Puritan Theology*, pp. 859-876.

[18] J. C. Ryle's influence is reflected in a 'modern English' update; Ryle, *Duties of Parents*.

[19] In our final chapter, we highlight a range of books and resources in this area.

[20] Full details of each resource are provided in the final chapter.

[21] Bengston, *Families and Faith,* pp 165-183. Bengston also notes that parental warmth – and especially a father's warmth – is key for helping children take on the faith of their parents, pp. 71-98. On the importance of parents and other adults for the faith of teenagers, see also Smith with Denton, *Soul Searching*, p. 267. For ways in which the church can encourage families in faith formation, see Gardner, *Mend the Gap*, esp. pp. 163-190.

[22] Bengston, *Families and Faith*, pp. 99-112.

[23] See the discussion of 'Prodigals' in Bengston, *Families and Faith*, pp. 131-144.

[24] Robert Wuthnow, 'Religious Upbringing', pp. 77-79.

Bibliography

Anthony, Michael and Michelle (eds.), *A Theology for Family Ministries*. Nashville, TN: B&H Publishing, 2011.

Bakke, O. M., *When Children Became People: The Birth of Childhood in Early Christianity*. Minneapolis: Fortress Press, 2005.

Beeke, Joel R. and Mark Jones, *A Puritan Theology: Doctrine for Life*. Grand Rapids, MI: Reformation Heritage Books, 2012.

Bengston, Vern L. with Norella M. Putney and Susan C. Harris, *Families and Faith: How Religion is Passed Down across Generations*. Oxford: Oxford University Press, 2013.

Bunge, Marcia J. (ed.), *The Child in Christian Thought*. Grand Rapids, MI: Wm B. Eerdmans Publishing Co., 2001.

Cooper, Barry, *Can I Really Trust the Bible?* Good Book Company, 2015.

DeYoung, Kevin, *Taking God at His Word: Why the Bible is worth knowing, trusting and loving*. Wheaton, Illinois: Crossway, 2014.

Evangelical Alliance, *21st Century Evangelicals: How's the Family?* London: Evangelical Alliance, 2012.

Gardner, Jason, *Mend the Gap: Can the Church Reconnect the Generations?* Nottingham: InterVarsity Press, 2008.

Garland, Diana R., *Family Ministry: A Comprehensive Guide,* 2nd ed. Downers Grove, IL: InterVarsity Press, 2012.

Gurion, Vigen, 'The Ecclesial Family: John Chrysostom on Parenthood and Children,' in *The Child in Christian Thought*, ed. Marcia J. Bunge, pp. 61-77.

Hellerman, Joseph H., *When the Church Was a Family: Recapturing Jesus' Vision for Authentic Christian Community*. Nashville, TN: B&H Publishing Group, 2009.

Jones, Timothy Paul and Randy Stinson, 'Family Ministry Models,' in *A Theology for Family Ministries,* ed. Michael and Michelle Anthony, pp. 155-180.

Jones, Timothy Paul and Randy Stinson (eds.), *Trained in the Fear of God*. Grand Rapids, MI: Kregel Publications, 2011.

Laistner, Max L. W., *Christianity and Pagan Culture in the Later Roman Empire*. Ithaca, NY: Cornell University Press, 1951.

Lawson, Michael S., 'Old Testament Teaching on the Family,' in *A Theology for Family Ministries*, ed. Michael and Michelle Anthony, pp. 66-87.

Melick Jr., Richard, 'New Testament Teachings on the Family,' in Michael & Michelle Anthony (eds.), *A Theology for Family Ministries,* pp. 88-105.

Ovey, Michael and Daniel Strange, *Confident: Why we can trust the Bible.* Ross-Shire: Christian Focus Publications, 2015.

Parker, Alison et al., *British Social Attitudes 28.* London: Sage Publications, 2012.

Ryle, J. C. *Duties of Parents,* edited into modern English by Alan Witchalls. Chorley: 10ofThose Publishing, 2013.

Smith, Christian with Melinda Lundquist Denton, *Soul Searching: The Religious and Spiritual Lives of American Teenagers.* Oxford: Oxford University Press, 2005.

Stanton, Graham, *Families – a Forgotten Factor?* Nottingham: Grove Books, 2011.

The Methodist Church, *We are Family: The Changing Nature of Family Ministry.* Methodist Publishing, 2015.

Wuthnow, Robert, 'Religious Upbringing: Does it Matter and, if so, what matters?' in *Christ and the Adolescent: A Theological Approach to Youth Ministry,* ed. James W. Fowler, Robin Mass and Robert Wuthnow. Princeton, N.J.: Institute for Youth Ministry, Princeton Theological Seminary, 1996, pp. 77-87.

'Whenever we open Scripture, even if Toby is throwing carrots across the table, God wants to speak to us.'

Contents

'We learn from our children's prayers, and are encouraged and challenged by their simple faith.'

Ed & Gareth: thank you to all the families who have opened their hearts and their homes to us, sharing stories (and photos) in the belief that family worship matters. It's been a huge privilege to talk with you all, and we pray that your stories – the heart of our book – would inspire others just as they have encouraged us. We pray that God would continue to bless you all.

Thank you, John, for being a partner in this project and for publishing our book. You caught our vision from the start, and have kept us honest with the challenges while also delighting us with your designs. We really couldn't have done this without you!

Thank you to all who put us in touch with others or helped us along the way, especially David & Maura, Ben and Duncan. Thanks to John and Jonathan for valuable insights into Christian marketing and publishing.

Ed: thanks, Gareth for helping with the book in the midst of other commitments; it's been great to have you a part of this! Thanks also to family and friends who have supported this project from the start, including all at Trinity Church.

Thank you, Ali; your endless support for my 'projects' knows no end and it's a joy to share with you the task of raising our boys. Thanks, Archie & Toby for putting up with my busy days at the desk; I love you guys so much, and know that one day you'll understand a little more about this book!

Gareth: thanks, Ed for inviting me onto this exciting and important project and for keeping us focused on the end goal! Thanks, Simon for encouraging the idea from the very beginning and allowing me to work on it amidst my 'normal' job.

Thank you, Sarah, my partner in raising our boys in the instruction of the Lord, thank you for all your encouragements, insights and ideas along the way on this project. Thanks to Ben, Tom and Luke who have taught me more about family worship than I could have read in any book and for sharing the most special time of our day together.

Copyright © 2016 Ed Mackenzie and Gareth Crispin

Written by Ed Mackenzie and Gareth Crispin
Designed and published by Morse-Brown Design www.morsebrowndesign.co.uk

ISBN: 978-1-907615-21-4

Unless otherwise stated, all Scripture quotations taken from the Holy Bible, New International Version Anglicised Copyright © 1979, 1984, 2011 Biblica. Used by permission of Hodder & Stoughton Ltd, an Hachette UK company.

Published by Morse-Brown Publishing.

Morse-Brown Publishing
The Bond, 180-182 Fazeley St.
Birmingham B5 5SE

T: +44 (0)121 212 9857
E: john@morsebrowndesign.co.uk
W: www.morsebrowndesign.co.uk

Together with God

AN INTRODUCTION TO FAMILY WORSHIP

ED MACKENZIE & GARETH CRISPIN

'*Together with God* is the biblical pattern for families – we're to meet together with God as we read His Word and turn it into prayer and worship. But the Bible doesn't spell out how to do it. That's where this book is unique, and hugely helpful. 15 families have invited us to join them as they meet together. Each family is different - and yours will be too - but between them they give us easy ideas to copy, creative approaches for when things feel a bit stale, and masses of encouragement to keep going, and to help the next generation grow to know and love the Lord for themselves.'

Alison Mitchell, author, *Beginning with God* series.

'Full of creative ideas, resources and inspiration for worshipping God as a family, this is a book that will help you nurture the faith of your children. Each story is a fascinating snapshot into the ways different families have found to engage in prayer and Bible reading together. I found it deeply moving, and it has challenged me to explore new ways of seeking God with my own daughters.'

Jo Swinney, co-author of *Keeping Faith: being family when belief is in question.*

PRAISE FOR TOGETHER WITH GOD

'*Together with God* is a rich resource to encourage family worship, chock full of ideas to help families of many varieties to meet together with God. I loved how it's rooted in real life, and how it addresses challenges as well as joys.'

Amy Boucher Pye, *Finding Myself in Britain.*

'An extremely useful book for those of us who struggle to know how best to pass our faith on to the next generation. It doesn't contain pie in the sky theory, but overflows with ideas that are actually being used by families. The families' stories of how they worship together are inspiring, encouraging and honest. Ed and Gareth have done a fantastic job of drawing them together and presenting a down-to-earth guide about a heavenly subject.'

Mark Chester, Founder, *Who Let the Dads Out?*

'These very personal stories, simply and honestly told by parents from a variety of backgrounds, create a lovely mosaic of family devotional times. Bookended by the biblical insights that begin the book, and the practical tips at the end, they are a real encouragement for families to just 'have a go."

Bob Hartman, author, *The Lion Storyteller Bible.*

'This book is packed with stories from everyday families and gives great ideas to help us all as we pass on our faith to our children. I loved reading this and know that you will too. Buy it and keep it in the kitchen to refer to and let your children read it too.'

Mark and Lindsay Melluish, authors of *Parenting Children; Regional Director, New Wine.*

continued...